AFRICAN Needlepoint Designs

CHARTED FOR EASY USE

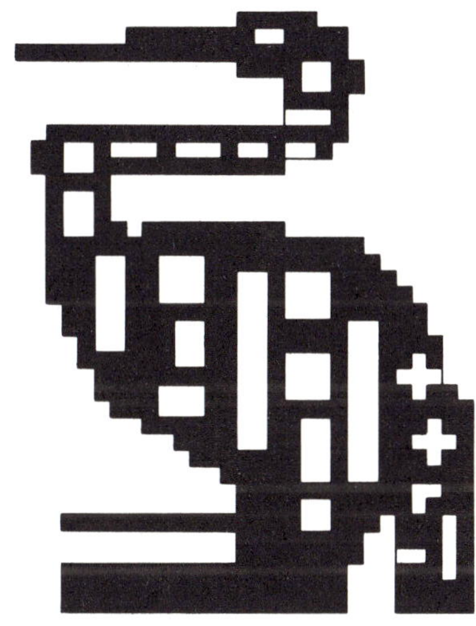

Diana Oliver Turner

DOVER PUBLICATIONS, INC.
NEW YORK

For Roland
and our children.

Published in Canada by General Publishing Company, Ltd., 30 Lesmill Road, Don Mills, Toronto, Ontario.

Published in the United Kingdom by Constable and Company, Ltd., 10 Orange Street, London WC 2.

African Needlepoint Designs is a new work, first published by Dover Publications, Inc., in 1976.

International Standard Book Number: 0-486-23244-1
Library of Congress Catalog Card Number: 75-21352

Manufactured in the United States of America
Dover Publications, Inc.
180 Varick Street
New York, N. Y. 10014

Introduction

Although the peoples of Africa have always had a highly developed sense of design, it is only fairly recently that their superb artifacts and handicrafts have been granted their just due in the form of widespread general acclaim. In the past few decades the original, sophisticated and varied designs from the Dark Continent have been the subject of numerous popular books and articles, while the craftwork itself has become widely collected by amateurs and professionals alike.

This particular collection of designs grew out of the enjoyable combination of my longtime interest in African art and my somewhat more recent addiction to needlepoint. For some time I have had the fun of challenging myself to adapt for needlepoint such strikingly different motifs as a highly stylized carved soapstone monkey from the Zimbabwe site in Rhodesia *(Page 2)* and a sophisticated geometric woven pattern on silk cloth from the Ashanti tribe in Ghana *(Page 26)*. My hobby became more of an obsession as this book took shape. In it I have tried to suggest the great richness and variety to be found in African art. My designs derive from the craftwork of 17 different countries, and reflect the African love of life, theater, and dance, respect for ritual, and concern with mortality.

I have found that these designs make up into handsome and much-appreciated gifts. Many lend themselves to personalization, which always adds a nice touch. For instance, when I did the headrest with the Luba design of an embracing couple *(Page 17)* as a wedding present, I stitched the names of the bride and groom above the motif and their wedding date below.

In the interest of authenticity, the colors that I have chosen for the designs in the color section, and those rendered in needlepoint and reproduced on the covers, correspond to the dye colors traditionally used in African textiles. The reader should, however, feel perfectly free to alter the color schemes according to his own taste.

It is a good idea to work out a complete, detailed color scheme for the design before beginning a project. You may find it more convenient to put tracing paper over the design and to experiment with colors on the tracing paper. In this way the design in the book will not be ruined if you decide to change the colors.

After you have worked out a color scheme, the design may be transferred to the canvas. Since the designs are planned for working on a #10 needlepoint canvas—each square in the grid representing one stitch to be taken on the canvas—the design may be worked directly onto the canvas by counting off on it the same number of warp and woof squares shown in the diagram. You may prefer to outline your design on the canvas itself. Since needlepoint canvas is almost transparent, you can lay it over the designs in the book and trace the pattern directly onto the canvas. If you decide to paint your design onto the canvas, use either a nonsoluble ink, acrylic paint thinned appropriately with water so as not to clog the holes in the canvas, or oil paint mixed with benzine or turpentine. Designs placed on the canvas can be colored in as an aid to the worker. Always make sure that your medium is waterproof. Felt tipped pens are very handy both for outlining or coloring in the design on the canvas, but check the labels carefully because not all felt markers are waterproof. Before beginning any project make certain that all paint, ink or marker is thoroughly dry.

There are two distinct types of needlepoint canvas, single-mesh and double-mesh. Double-mesh is woven with two horizontal and two vertical threads forming each mesh whereas single-mesh is woven with one vertical and one horizontal thread forming each mesh. Double-mesh is a very stable canvas on which the threads will stay securely in place as you work. Single-mesh canvas, which is more widely used, is a little easier on the eyes because the spaces are slightly larger.

A tapestry needle with a rounded, blunt tip and an elongated eye is used for needlepoint. The most commonly used needle for a #10 canvas is the #18 needle. The needle should clear the hole in the canvas without spreading the threads. Special yarns which have good twist and are sufficiently heavy to cover the canvas are used for needlepoint.

Although there are over a hundred different needlepoint stitches, the one that is universally considered to be "the" needlepoint stitch is the *Tent Stitch,* an even, neat stitch that always slants upward from left to right across the canvas. The stitches fit very neatly next to their neighbors and form a hard finish with the distinctive look that belongs to needlepoint. The three most familiar variations of Tent Stitch are: Plain Half-Cross Stitch, Continental Stitch and Basket Weave or Diagonal Stitch. The choice of stitch has a great deal to do with the durability of the finished product.

Plain Half-Cross Stitch, while it does not cover the canvas as well as the other two variations, provides the most economical use of yarn. It uses about one yard of yarn for a square inch of canvas. The stitch works up quickly, but it has a tendency to pull out of shape, a disadvantage that can be corrected in blocking. This stitch should only be used for pictures, wall hangings and areas that will receive little wear. It must be worked on a double-mesh canvas.

Continental Stitch, since it covers the front and back of the canvas, requires more wool than the Plain Half-Cross Stitch (it uses about 1¼ yards of yarn to cover a square inch of fabric). The stitch works up with more thickness on the back than on the front. As a result the piece is more attractive with better wearing ability. This is an ideal stitch for tote bags, belts, headbands, upholstery and rugs since the padding on the reverse saves wear on the needlepoint. The Continental Stitch also pulls the canvas out of shape, but this is easily corrected by blocking.

The Basket Weave or Diagonal Stitch makes an article that is very well padded and will wear well. It uses the same amount of wool as the Continental Stitch and does not pull the canvas out of shape. Since the stitch is actually woven into the canvas, it reinforces the back. This stitch is especially suited for needlepoint projects that will receive a great deal of wear, such as chair seats and rugs. Its disadvantage is that it lacks maneuverability and is hard to do in areas where there are small shapes or intricate designs.

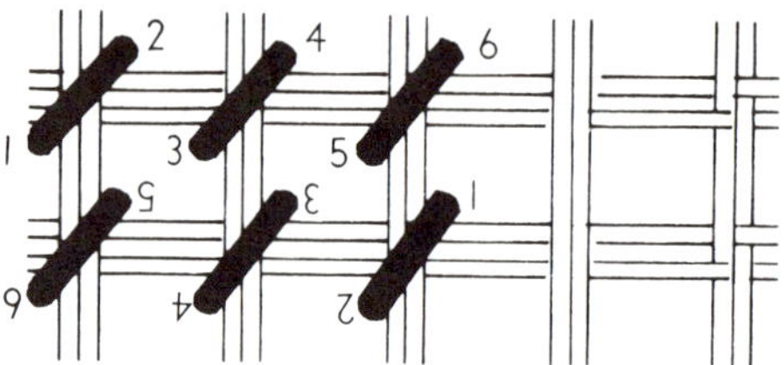

Plain Half-Cross Stitch: Always work Half-Cross Stitch from left to right, then turn the canvas around and work the return row, still stitching from left to right. Bring the needle to the front of the canvas at a point that will be the bottom of the first stitch. The needle is in a vertical position when making the stitch. Keep the stitches loose for minimum distortion and good coverage.

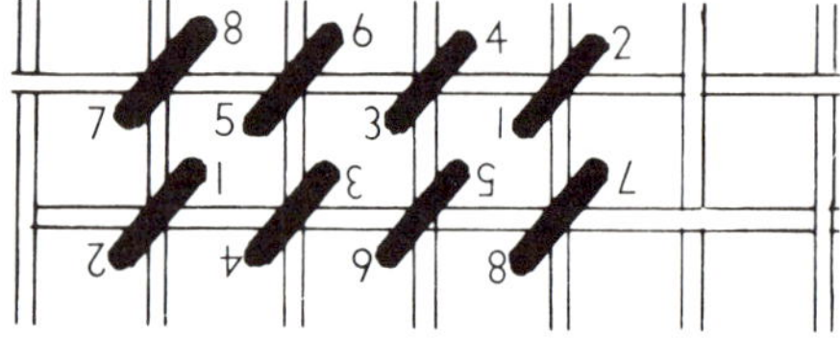

Continental Stitch: Start this design at the upper right-hand corner and work from right to left. The needle is slanted and always brought out a mesh ahead. The resulting stitch is actually a Half-Cross Stitch on top and a slanting stitch on the back. When the row is finished, turn the canvas around and work the return row, still stitching from right to left.

Basket Weave or Diagonal Stitch: Start the Basket Weave in the top right-hand corner *(left-handed workers should begin at the lower left).* Work the rows diagonally from left to right and then up the canvas from right to left. The rows must be alternated properly or a faint ridge will show where the pattern has been interrupted. Always stop working in the middle of a row rather than at the end so you will know in what direction your are working.

When starting a project, allow at least a 2″ margin of plain canvas around the needlepoint. Bind all the raw edges of the canvas with masking tape, double-fold bias tape or even adhesive tape. There are no set rules on where to begin a design. Generally it is easier to begin close to the center and work outward toward the edges of the canvas, working the backgrounds or borders last. To avoid fraying the yarn, work with strands not longer than 18″.

When you have finished your needlepoint, it should be blocked. No matter how straight you have kept your work, blocking will give it a professional look.

Any hard, flat surface that you do not mind marring with nail holes and one that will not be warped by wet needlepoint can serve as a blocking board. A large piece of plywood, an old drawing board or an old-fashioned doily blocker are ideal.

Moisten a Turkish towel in cold water and roll the needlepoint in the towel. Leaving the needlepoint in the towel overnight will insure that both the canvas and the yarn are thoroughly and evenly dampened. Do not saturate the needlepoint! Never hold the needlepoint under the faucet as this much water is not necessary.

Mark the desired outline on the blocking board, making sure that the corners are straight. Lay the needlepoint on the blocking board, and tack the canvas with thumbtacks about ½″ to ¾″ apart. It will probably take a good deal of pulling and tugging to get the needlepoint straight, but do not be afraid of this stress. Leave the canvas on the blocking board until thoroughly dry. Never put an iron on your needlepoint. You cannot successfully block with a steam iron because the needlepoint must dry in the straightened position. You may also have needlepoint blocked professionally. If you have a pillow made, a picture framed, or chair seat mounted, the craftsman may include the blocking in his price.

Your local needlepoint shop or department where you buy your materials will be happy to help you with any problems.

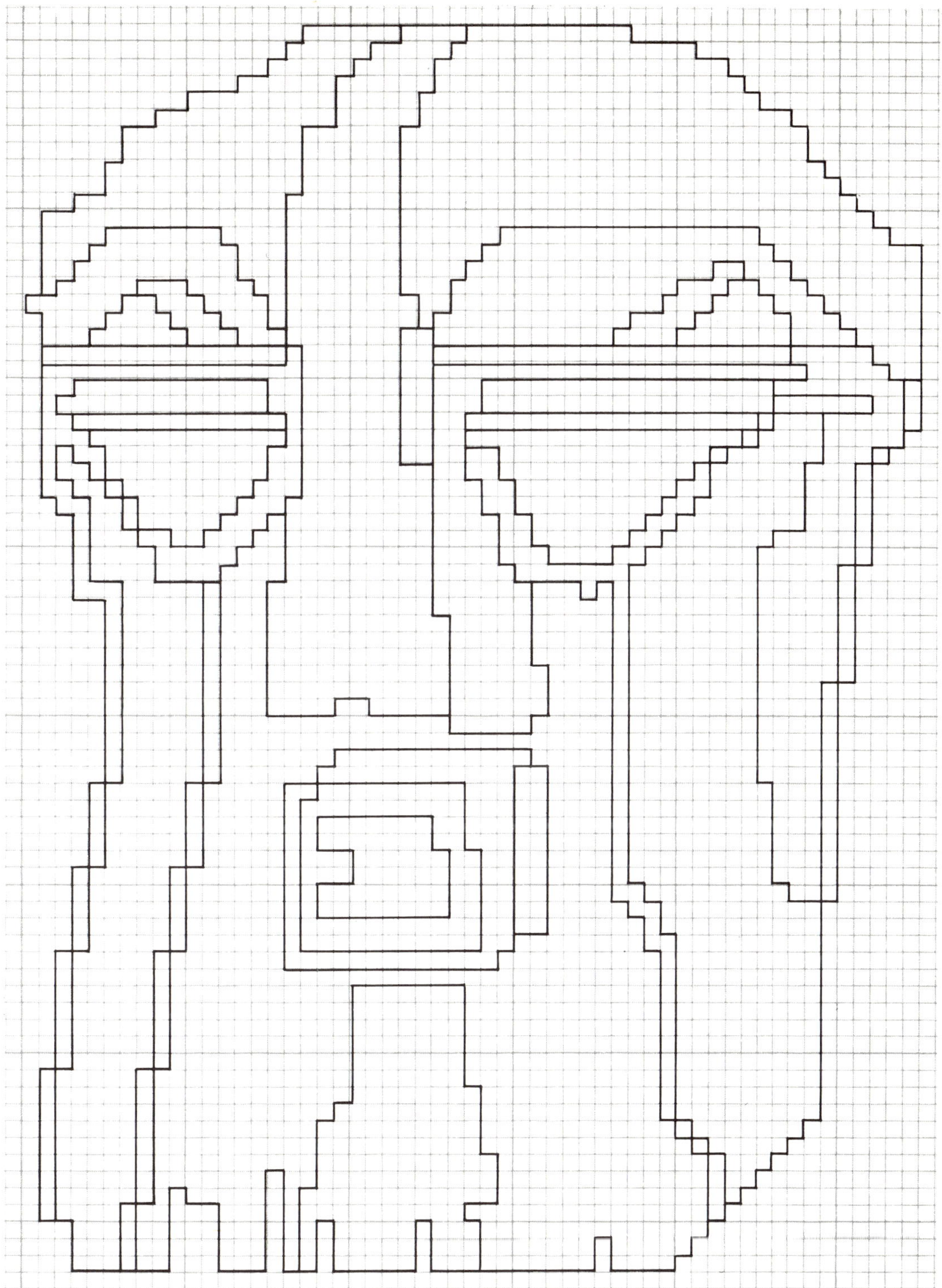

Mask (Kifwebe). Luba. Zaïre.

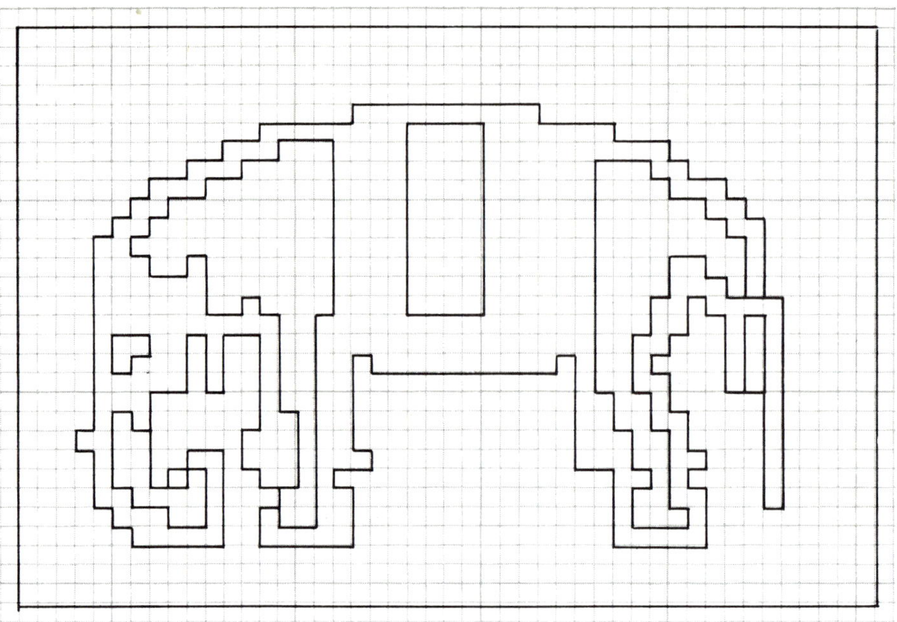

Elephant design on hide fan. Benin, Nigeria.

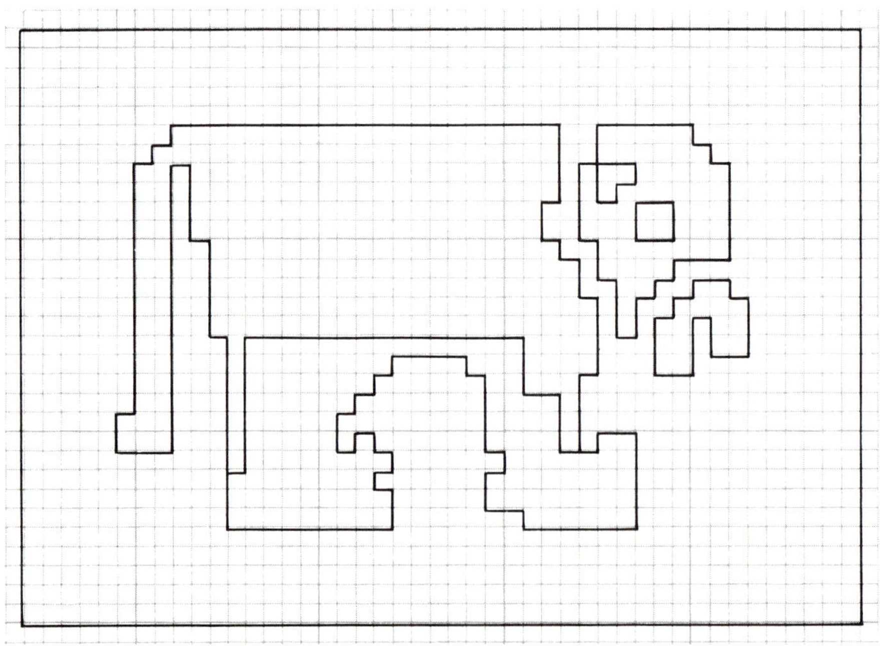

Carved soapstone monkey design from Zimbabwe, Rhodesia.

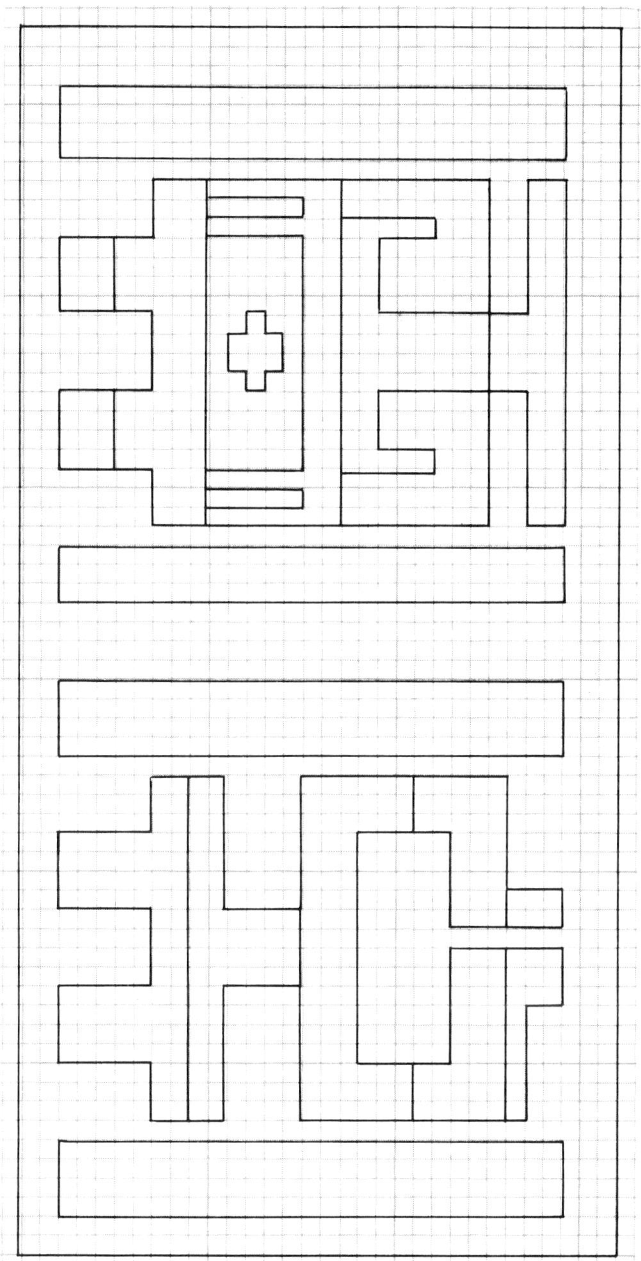

Beadwork design on apron. Ndebele. Republic of South Africa.

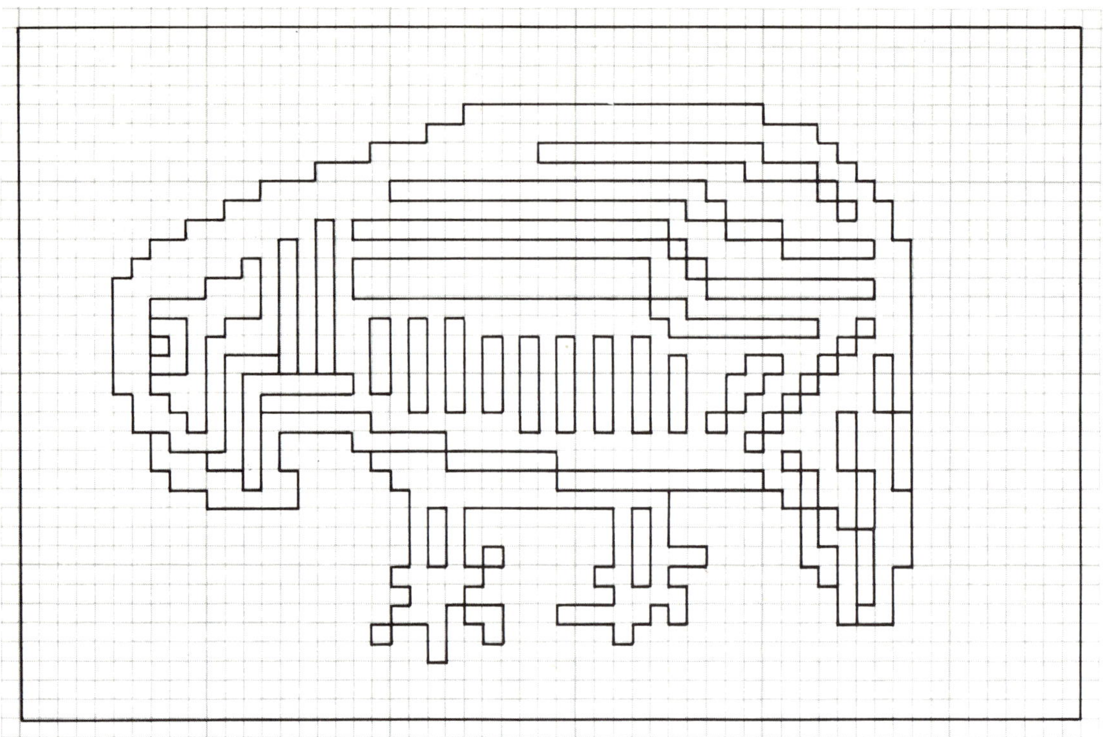

Brass repoussé bird design on an urn. Ashanti. Ghana.

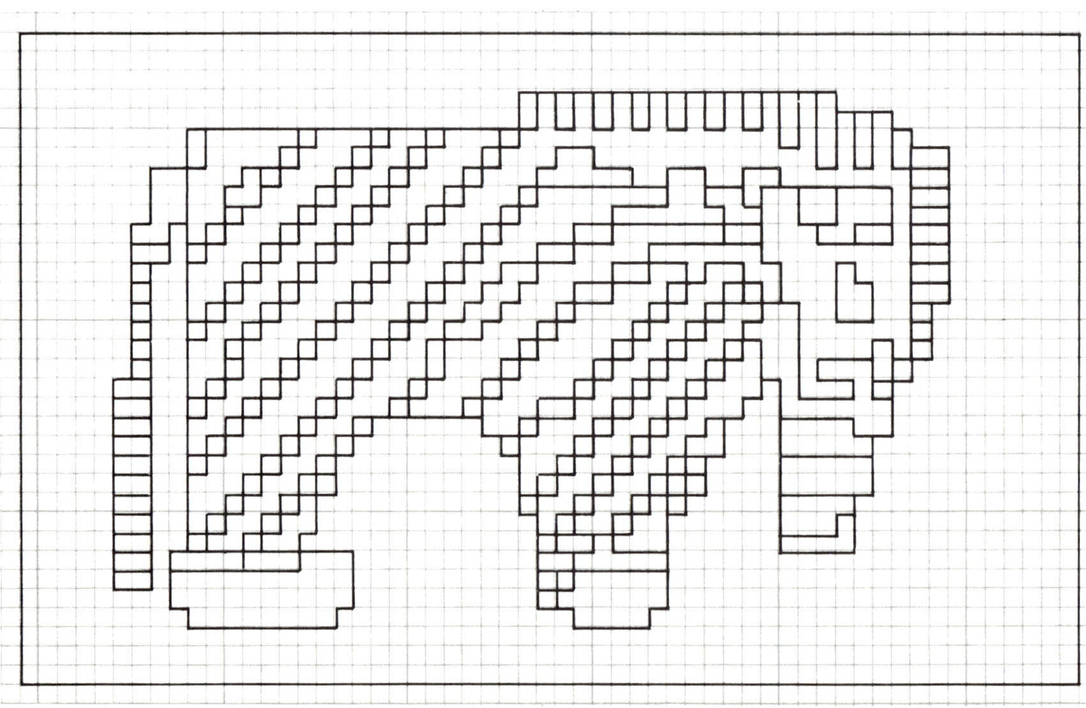

Carved soapstone zebra from Zimbabwe, Rhodesia.

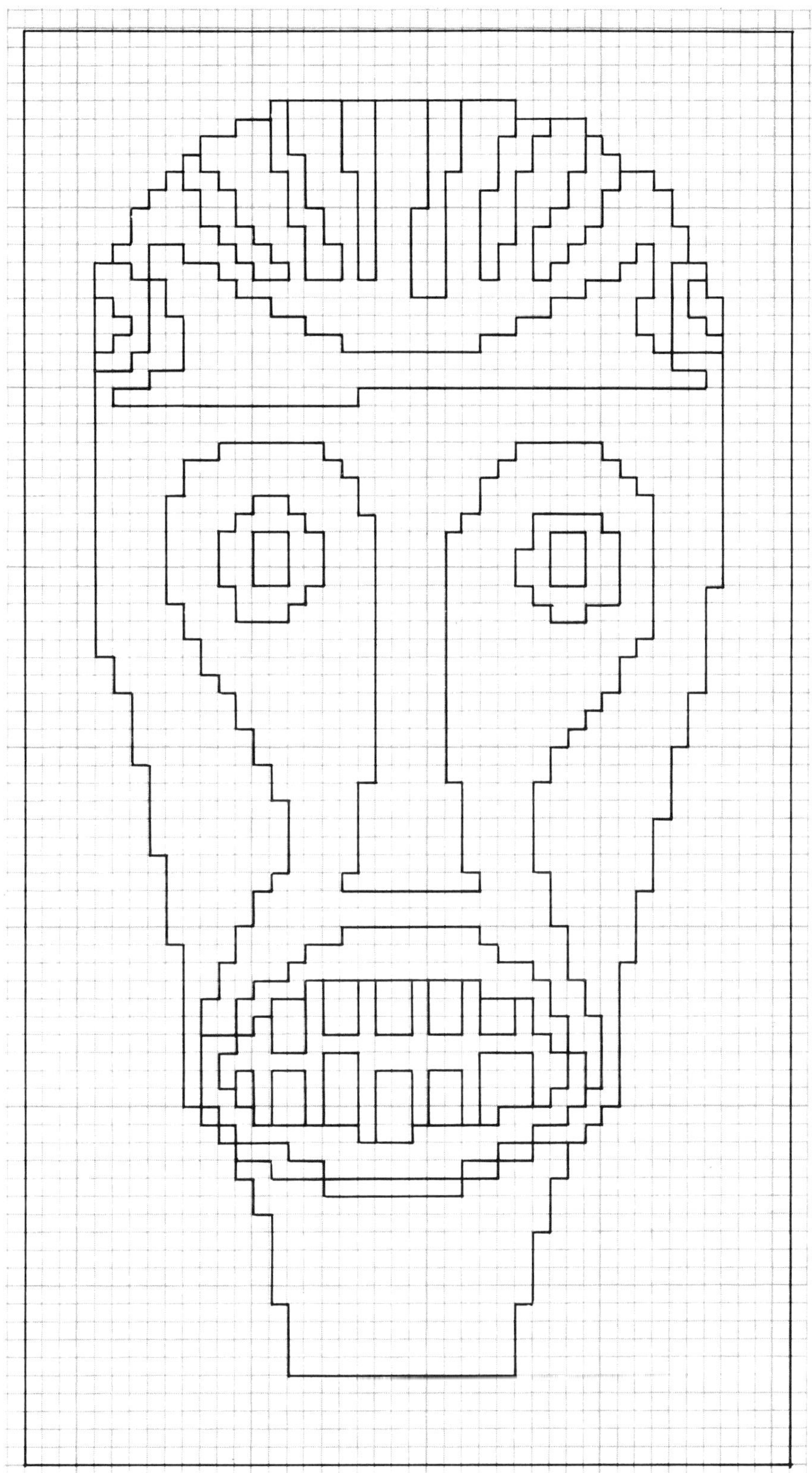

Painted wooden mask. Bafo. Cameroon.

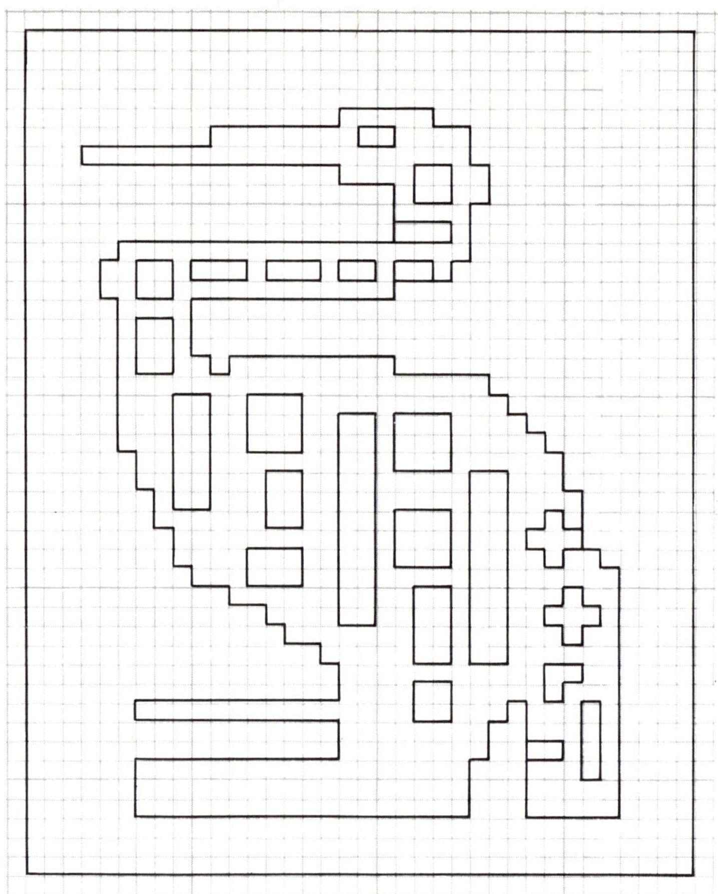

Scraped calabash bird design on drinking vessel. Dahomey.

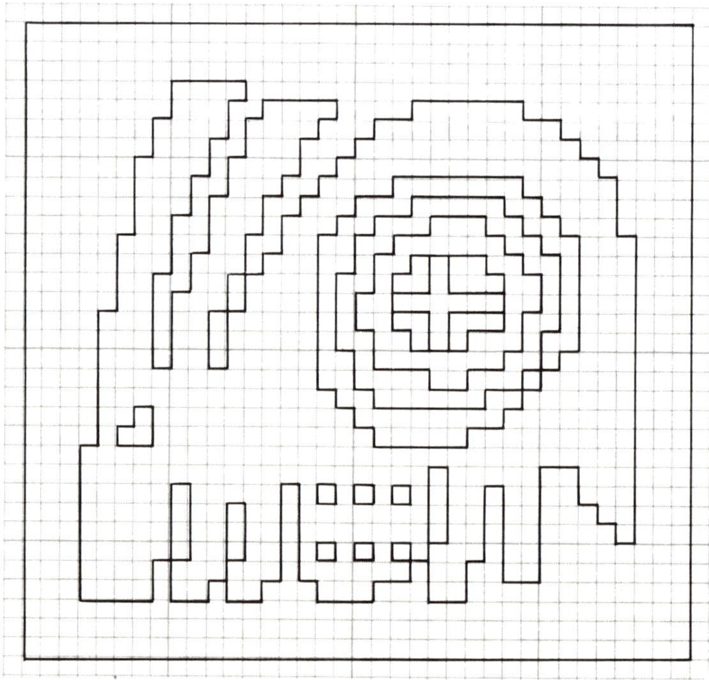

Scraped calabash cattle design. Dahomey.

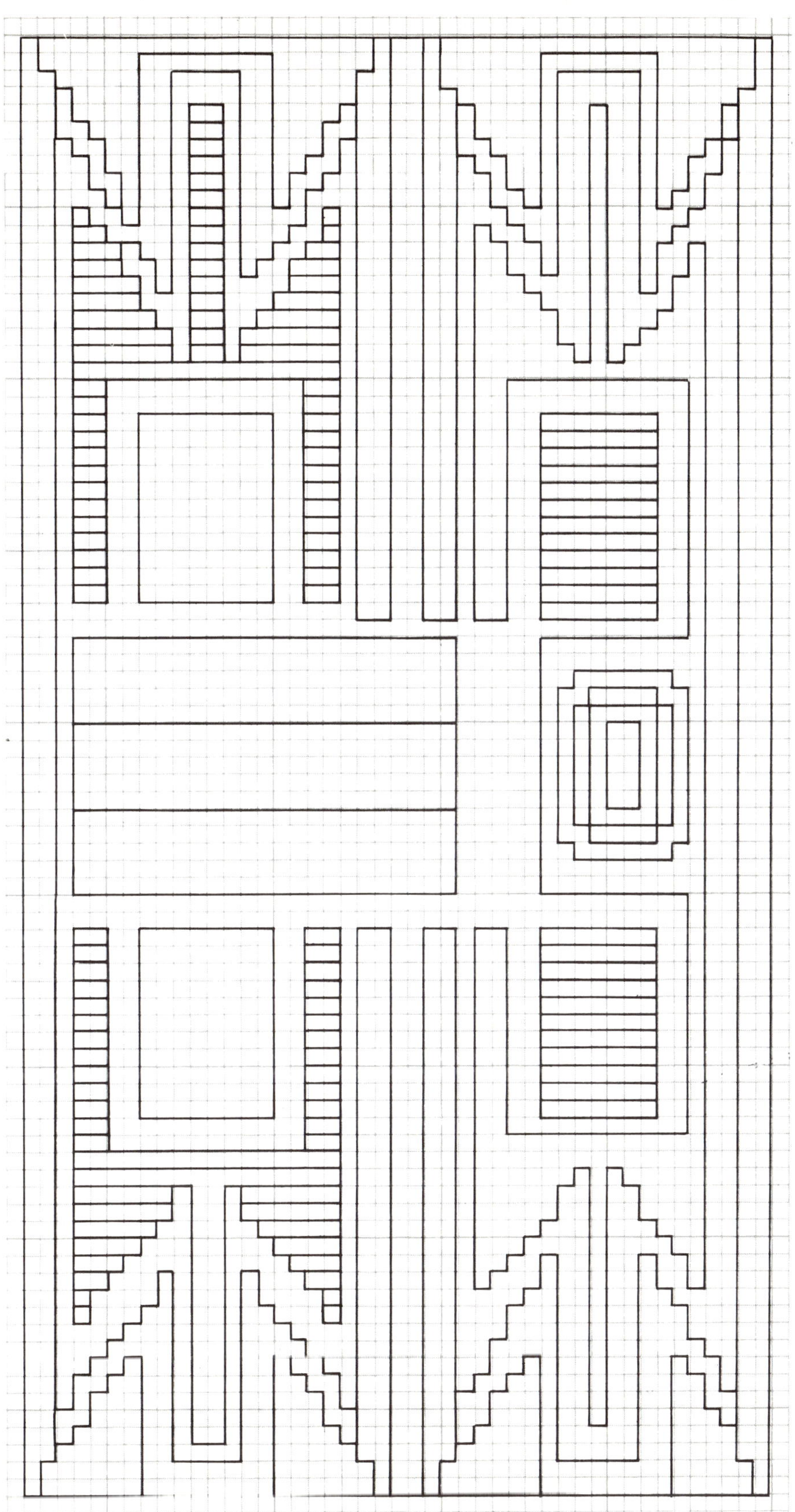

Painted wall facade. Ndebele. Republic of South Africa.

Carved design on wooden door latch. Dogon. Mali.

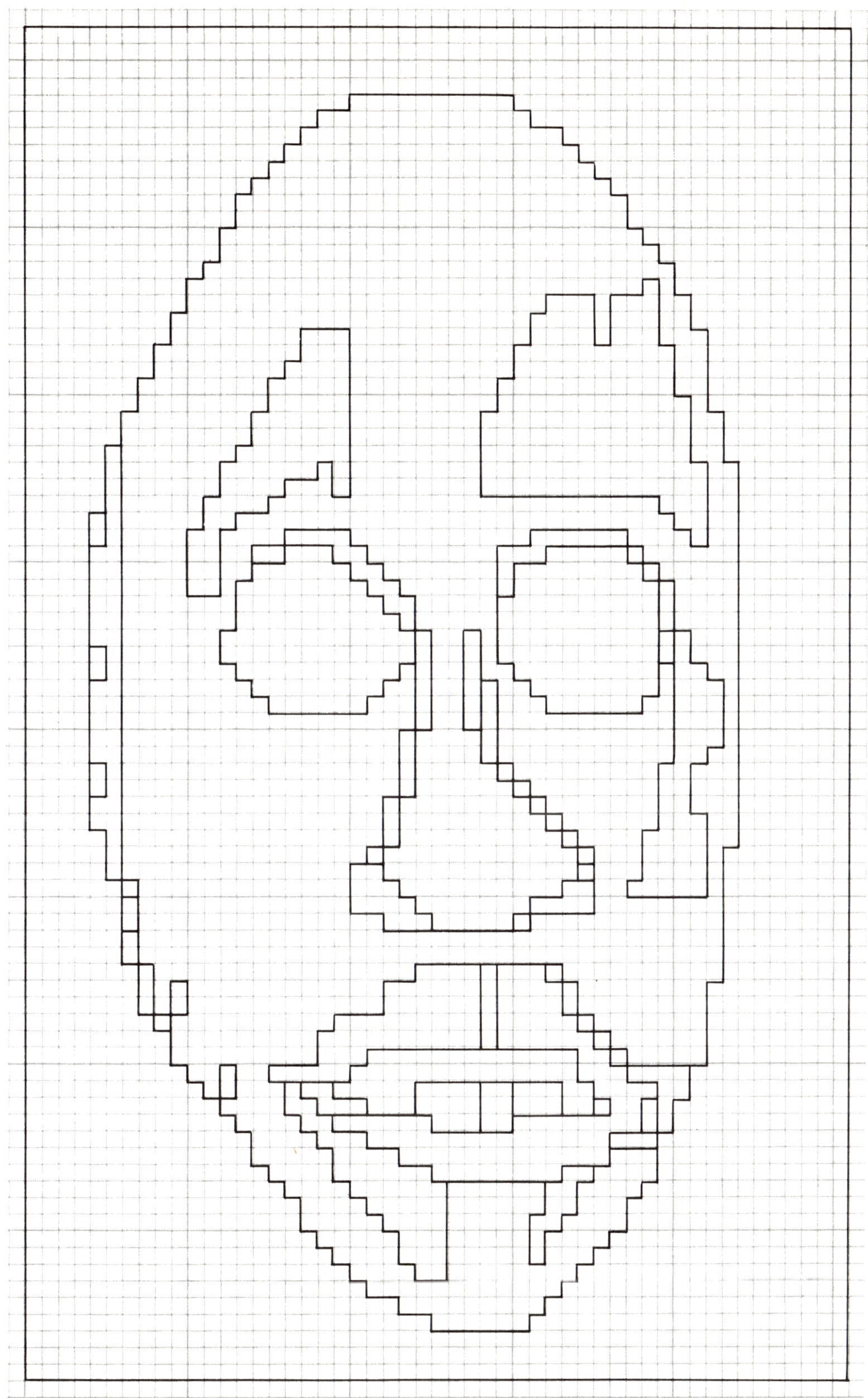

Mask. Dan. Ivory Coast.

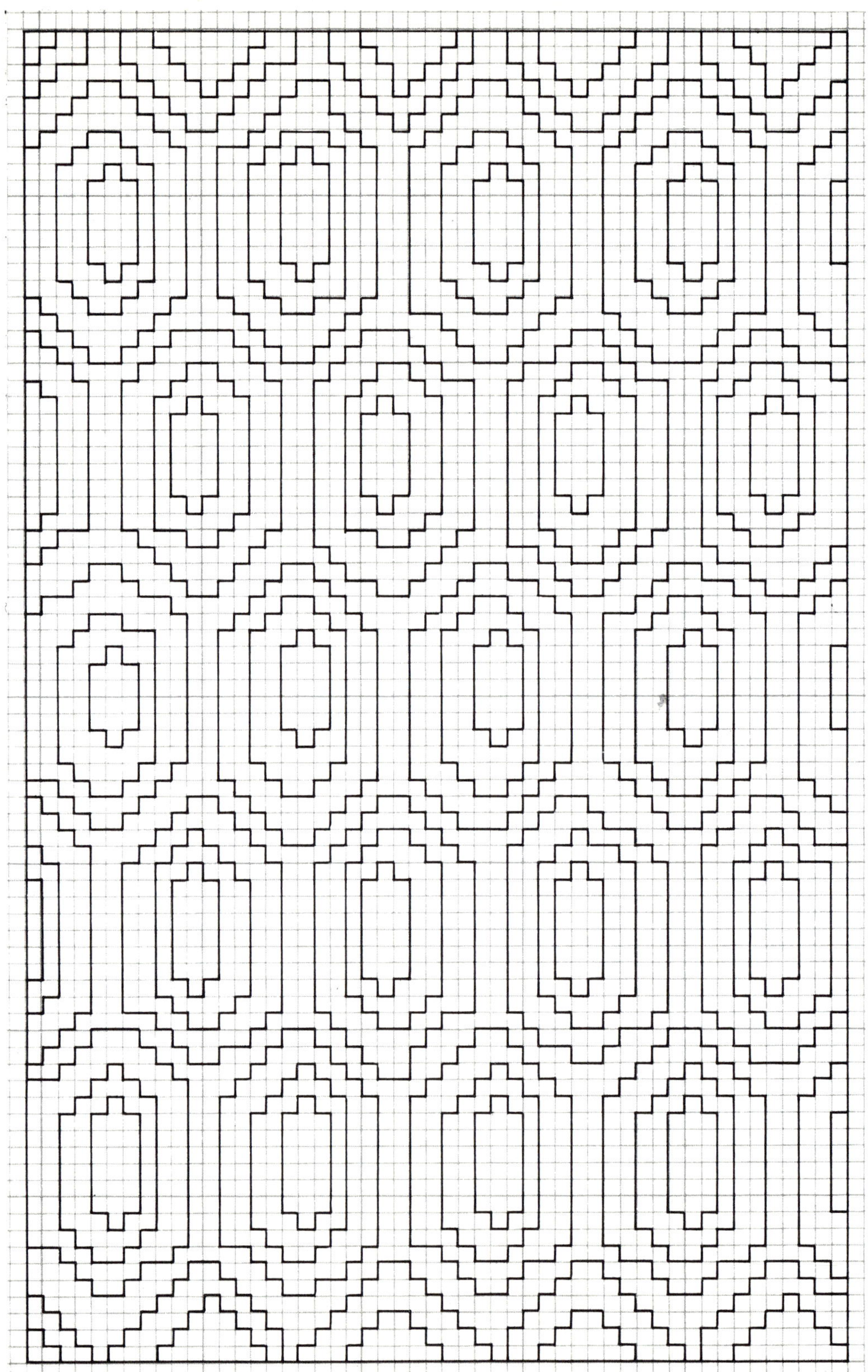

Raffia velour pattern. Kuba. Zaïre.

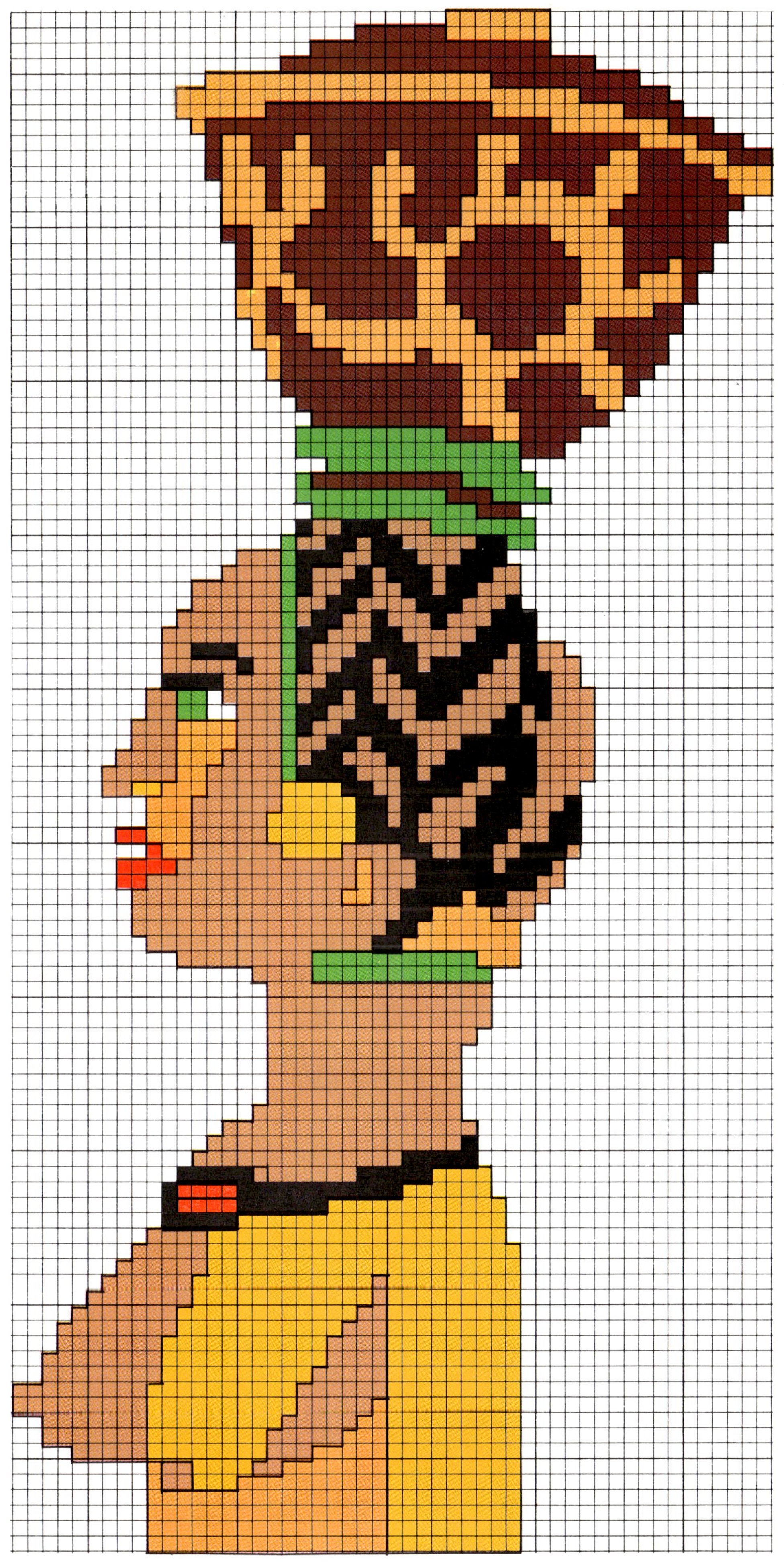

Head detail from wooden fertility sculpture. Baga. Guinea.

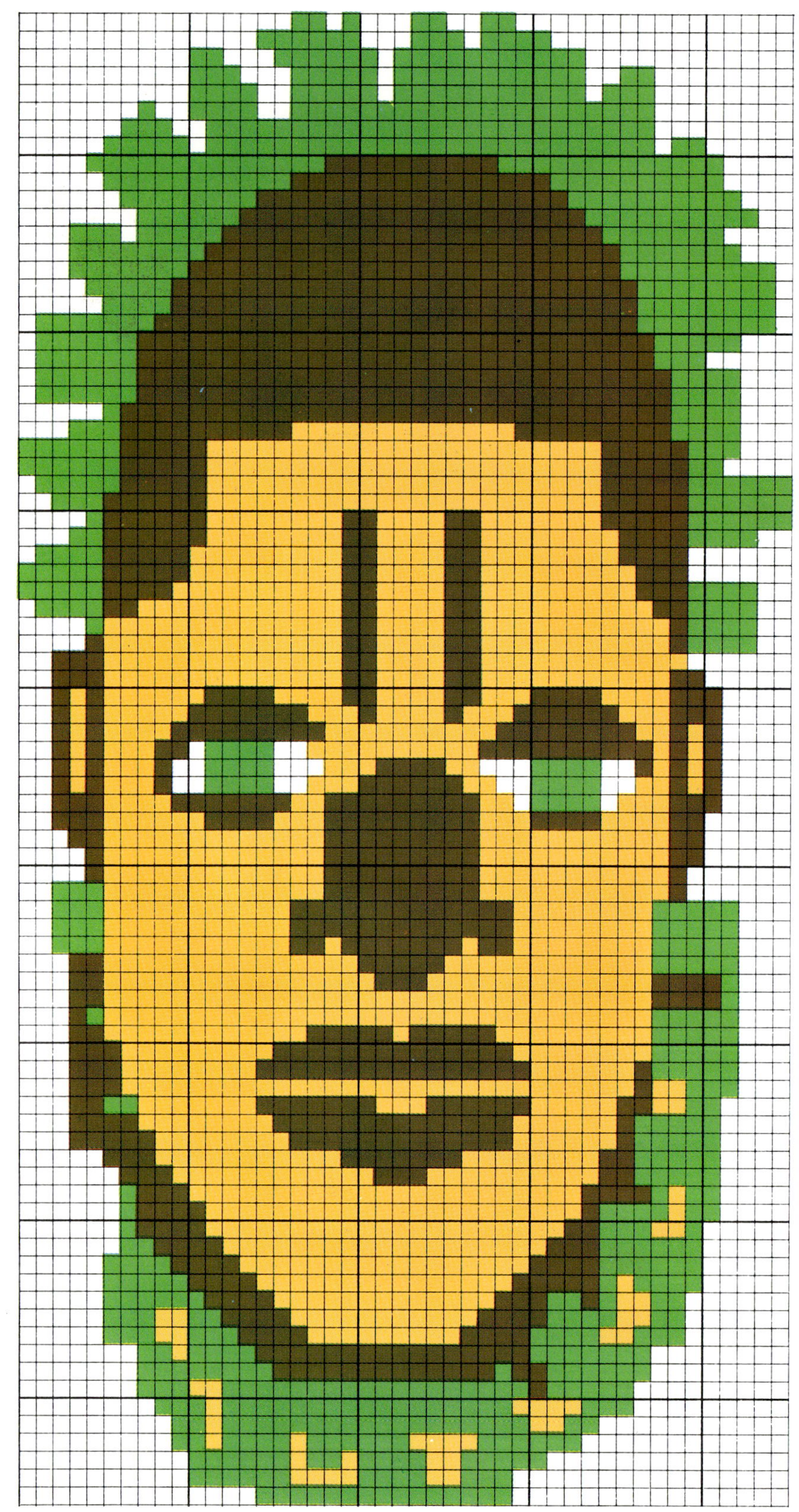

Pectoral mask. Benin, Nigeria.

Cast bronze gold weight. Ashanti. Ghana.

"Adinkira" printing stamp. Ashanti. Ghana.

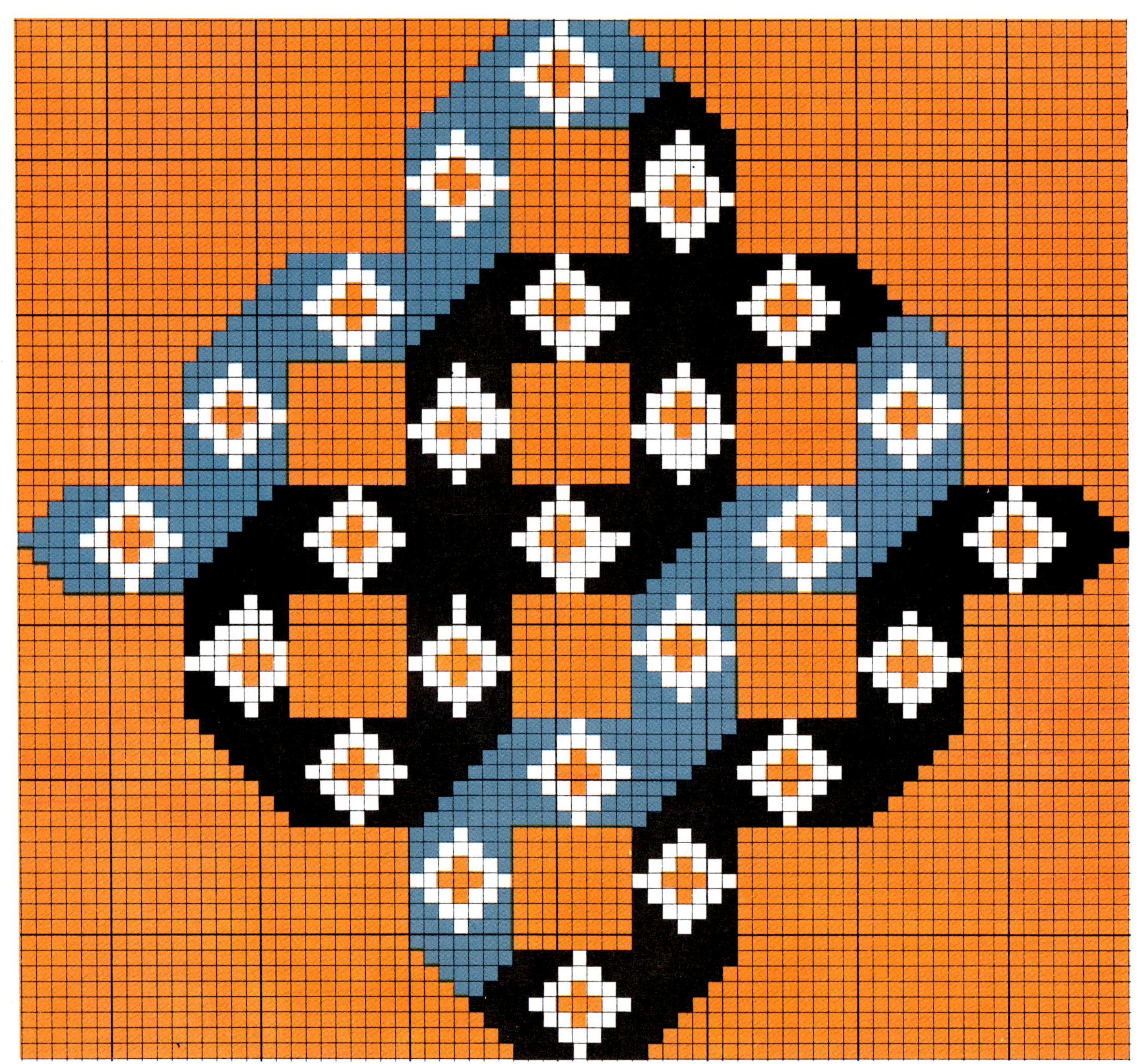

Plaited mat pattern. Zanzibar, Tanzania.

Mask. Bwaka. Zaïre

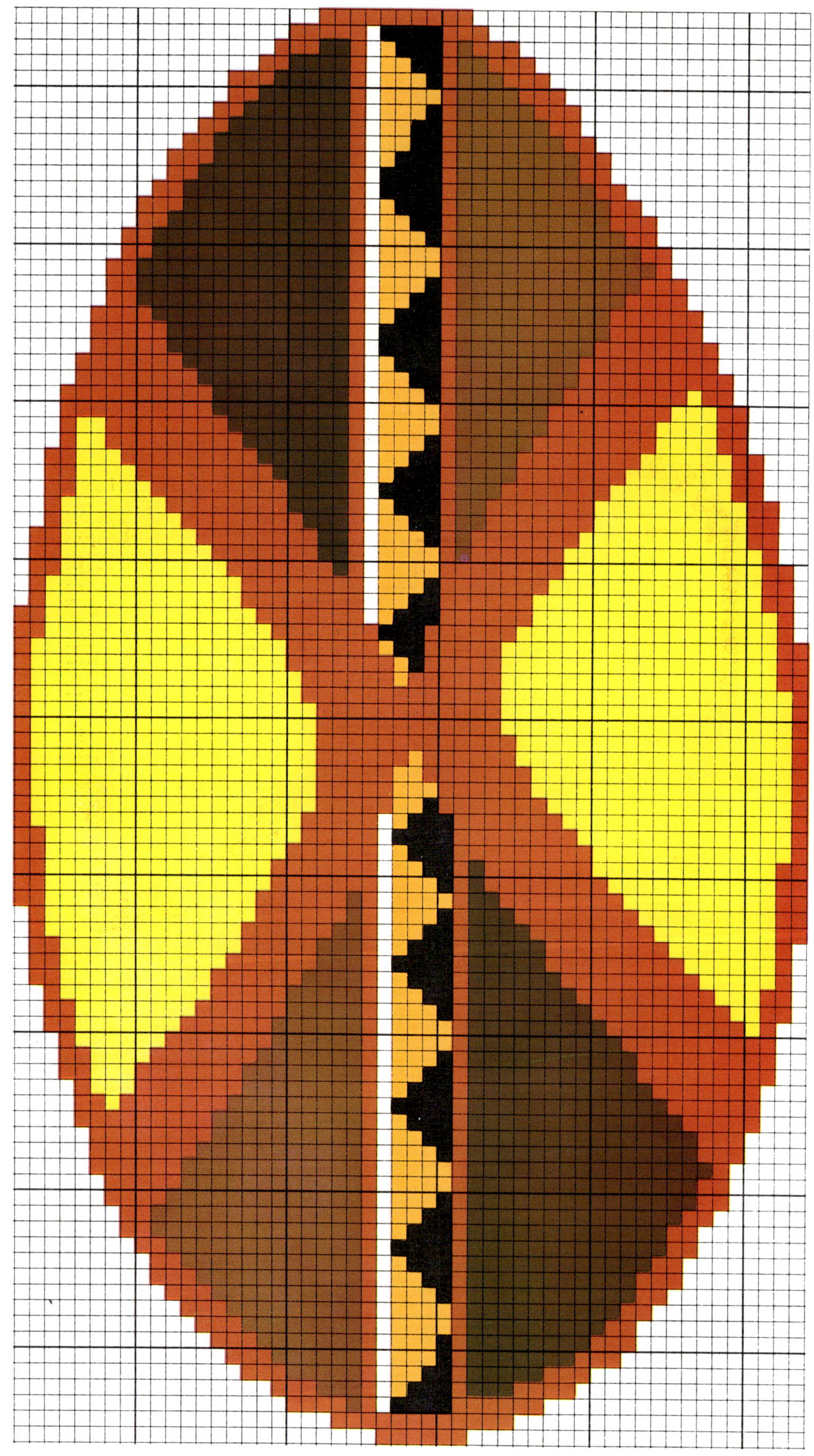

Painted hide shield. Masai. Kenya.

Head-rest with two figures. Luba. Zaïre.

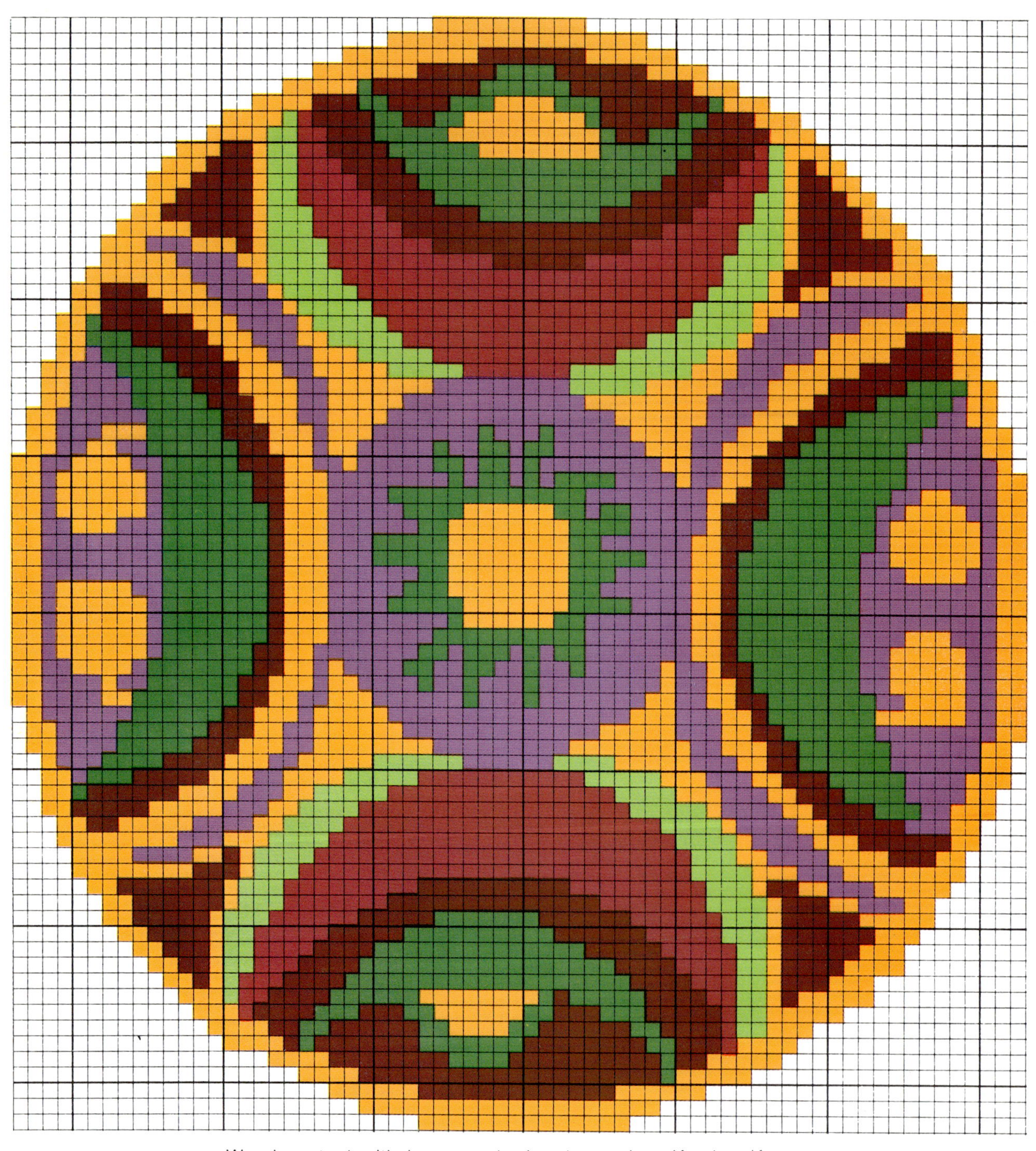

Wooden stool with hammered wire decoration. Kamba. Kenya.

Polychromed wooden mask. Bateké. Republic of the Congo.

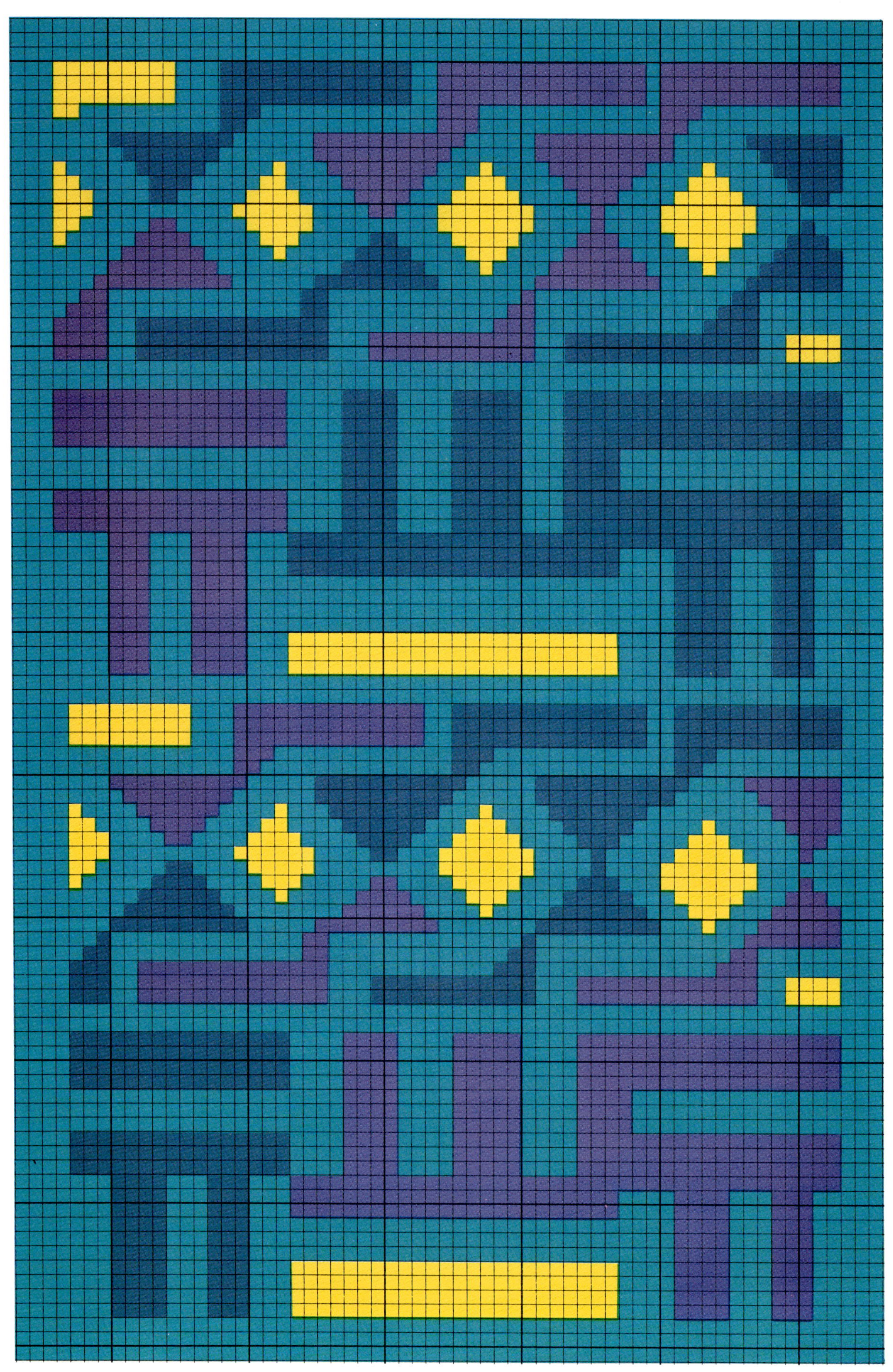

Embroidered cloth designs. Bushongo. Zaïre.

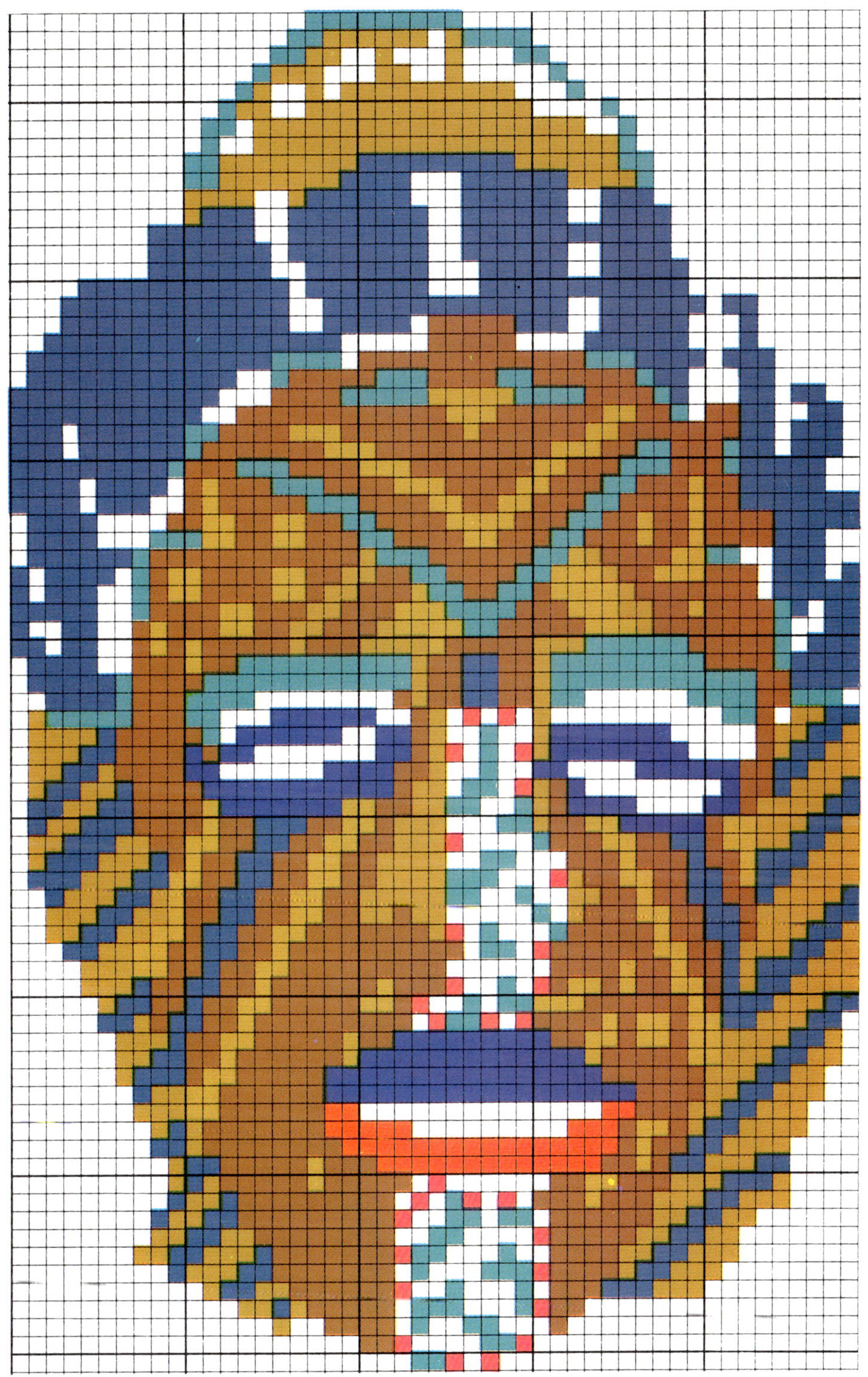

Dance mask. Kuba. Zaïre.

Tufted cloth pattern Zaïre.

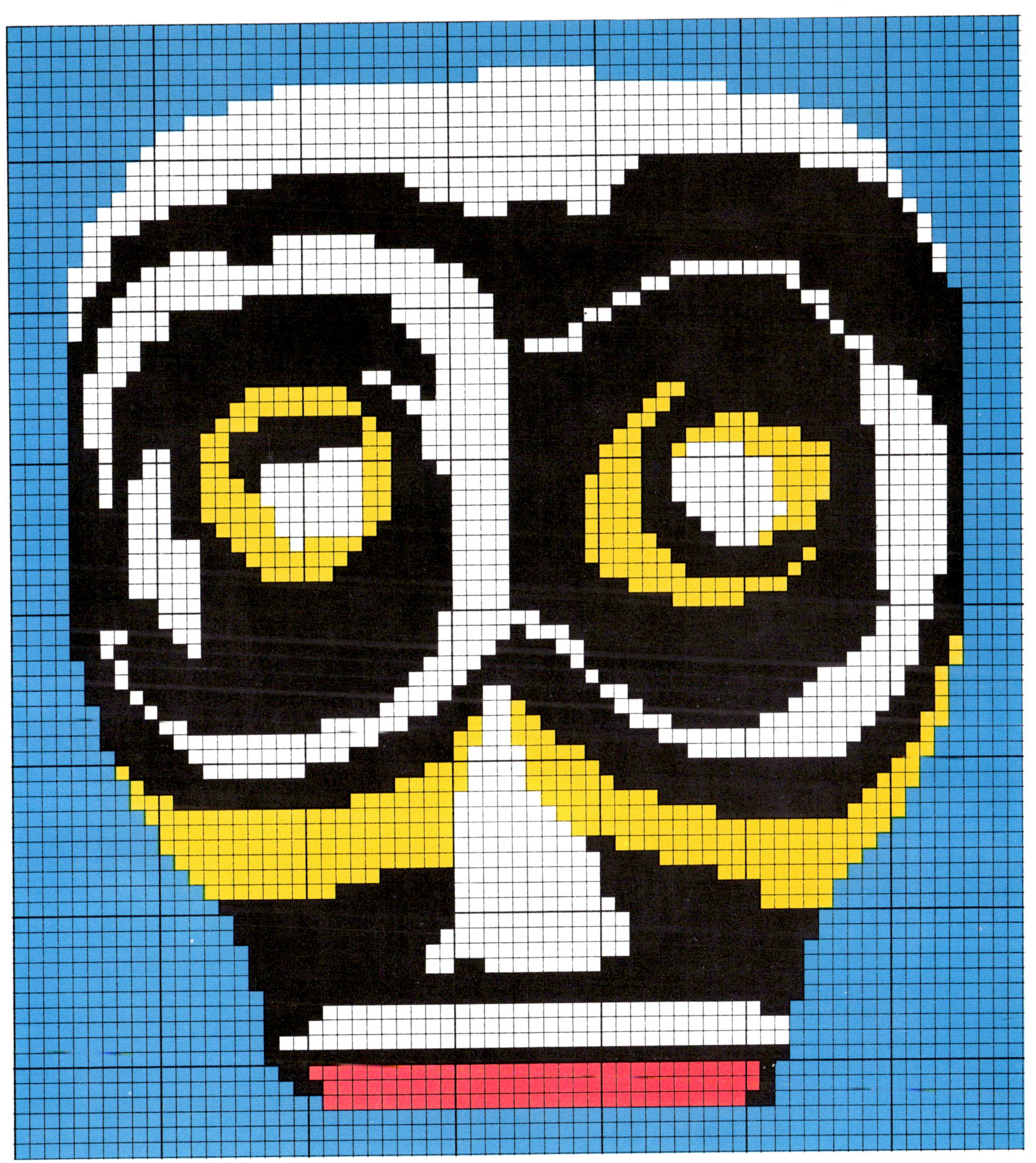

Mask. Ibo. Nigeria.

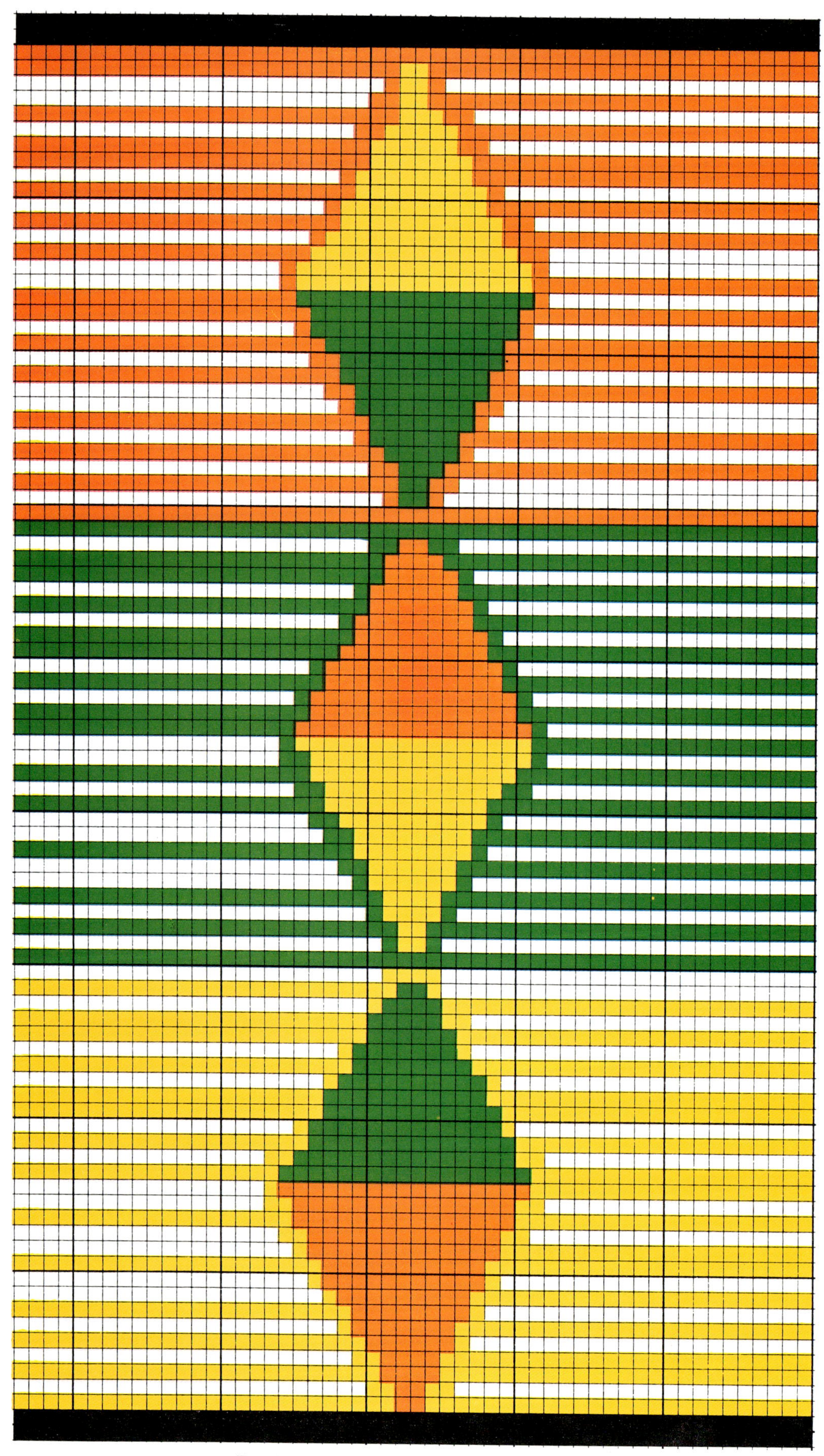

Bead apron design. Tswana. Botswana.

Woven mat design. Sundi. Republic of the Congo.

Cast bronze gold weight. Ashanti. Ghana.

Woven silk cloth. Ashanti. Ghana.

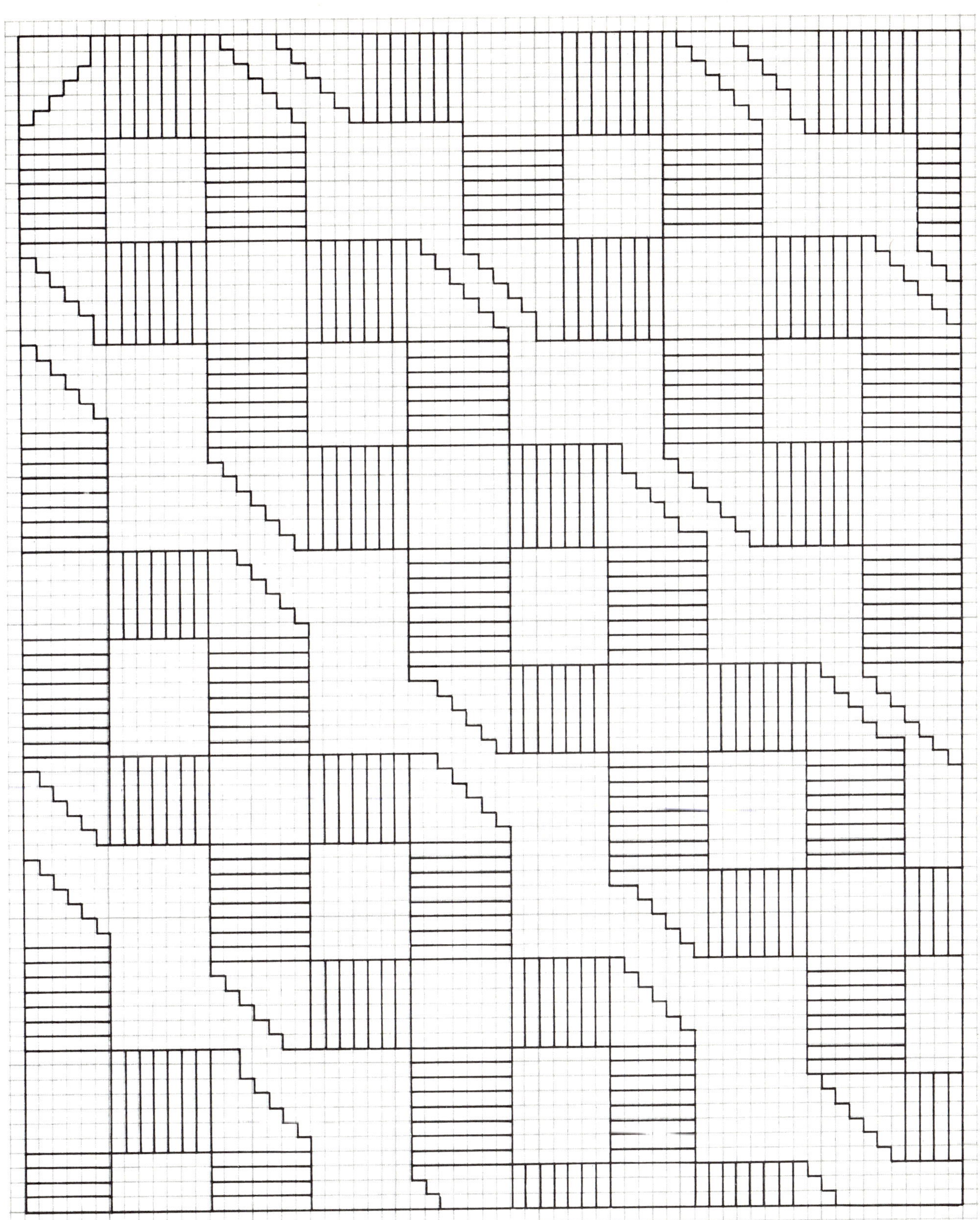

Carved design on a wooden divination vessel. Yoruba. Nigeria.

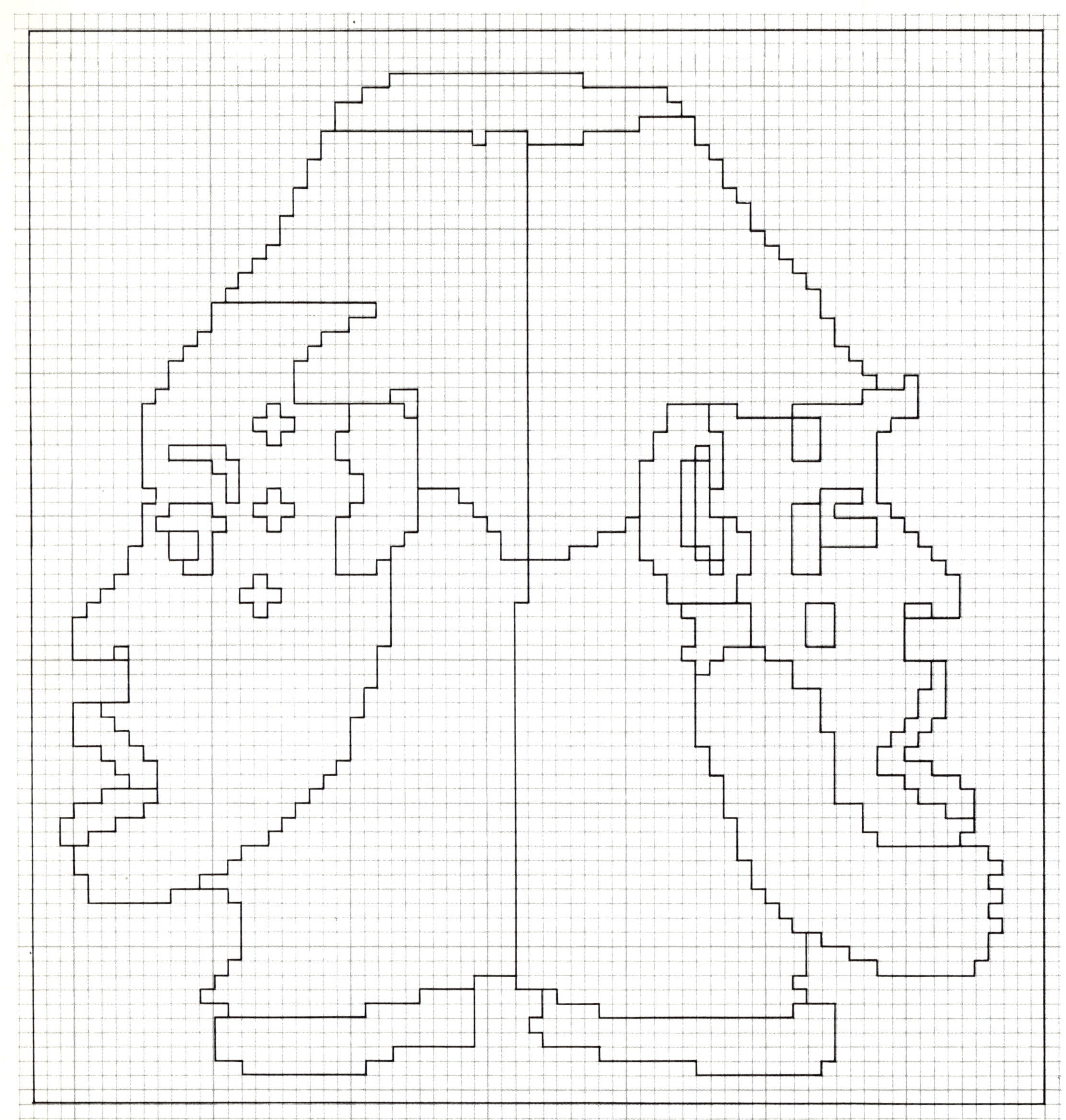

Janiform headdress mask. Ekoi. Cameroon.

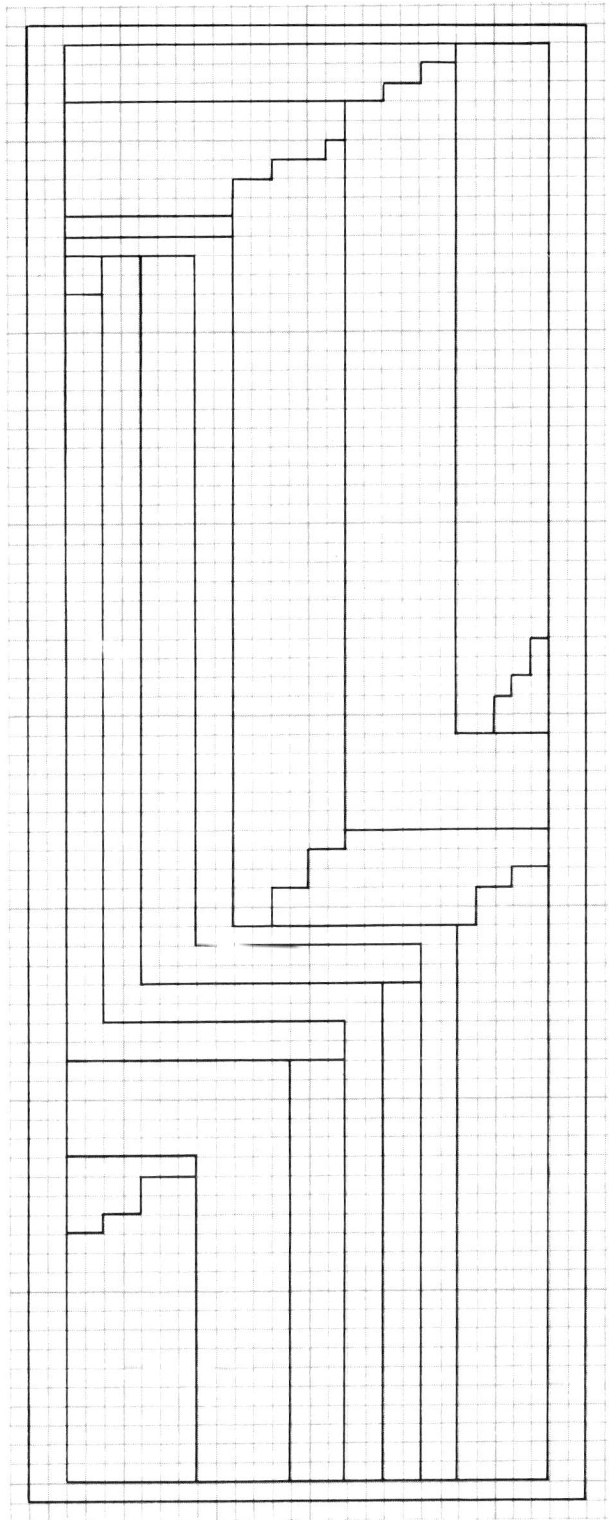

Hut screen. Tusi. Rwanda.

Sewn raffia mat pattern. Bushongo. Zaïre.

Detail of wall painting. Bangba. Zaïre.

Elephant spirit headdress symbolizing violence and ugliness for Ekkpe play. Benin, Nigeria

Maiden spirit headdress symbolizing beauty and kindness for Ekkpe play. Benin. Nigeria.

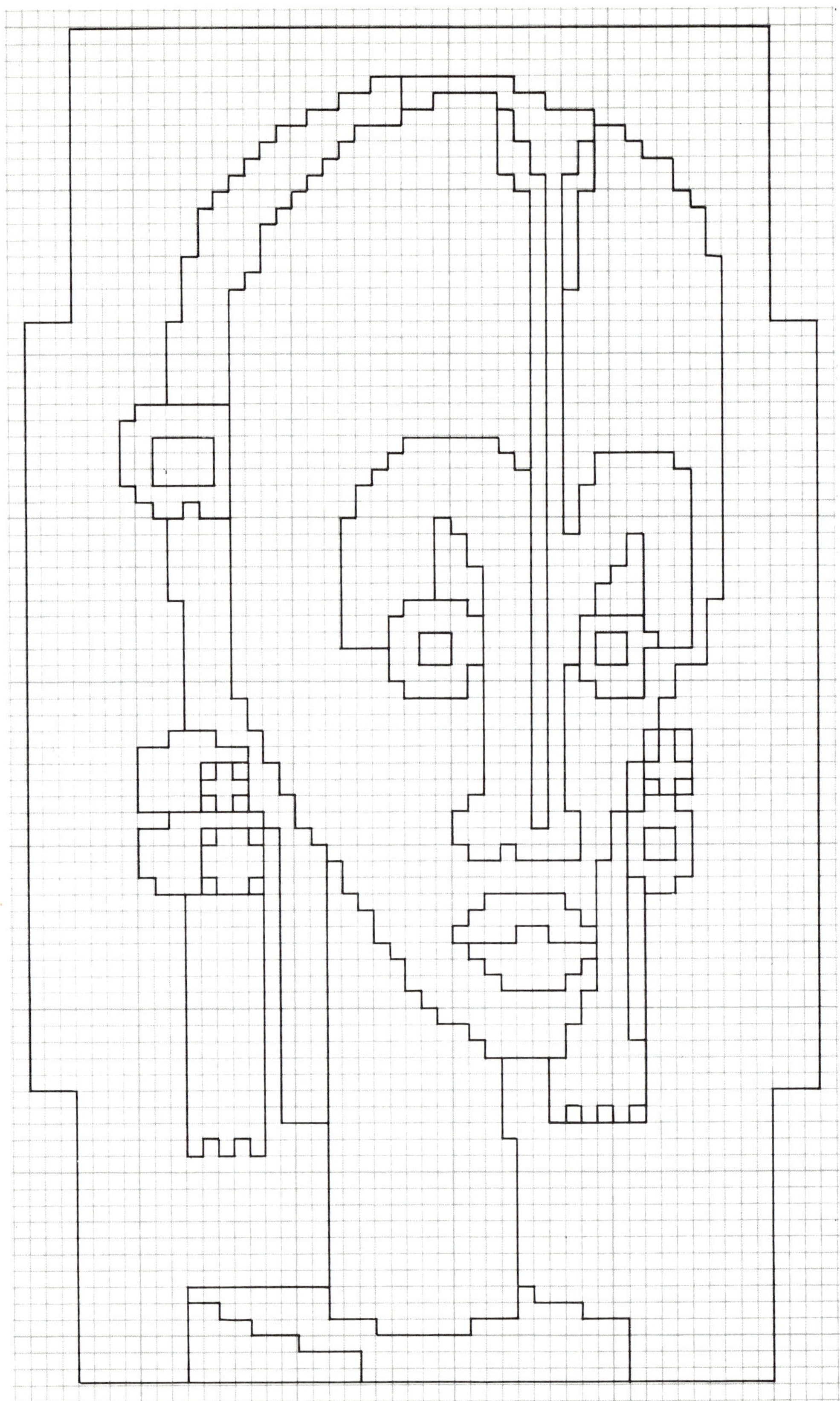

Reliquary head, carved to stand above receptacle containing the bones of ancestors. Fang. Gabon.

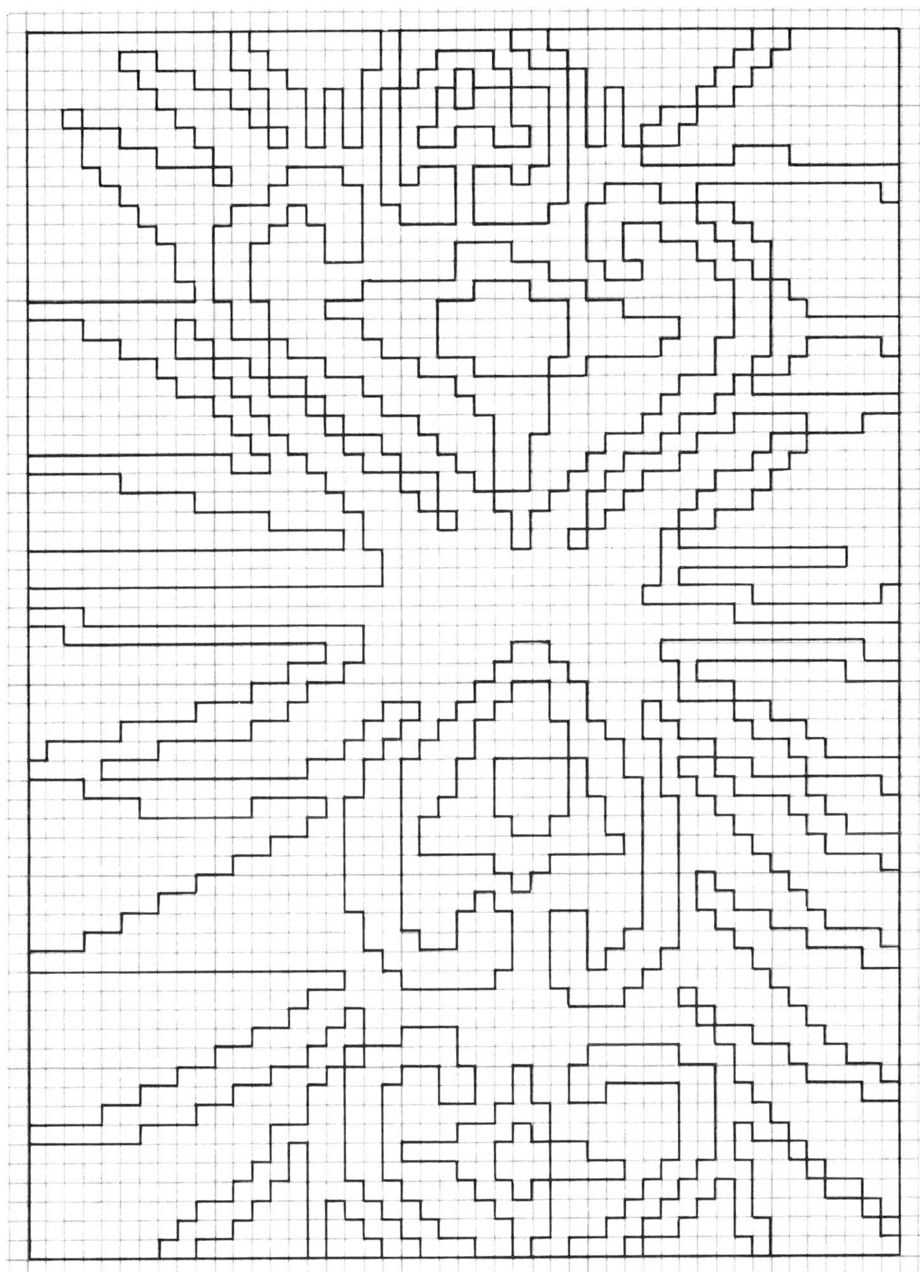

Wall painting. Luo. Kenya.

Bronze mask worn at the belt. Benin, Nigeria.

Mask. Bobo. Upper Volta.

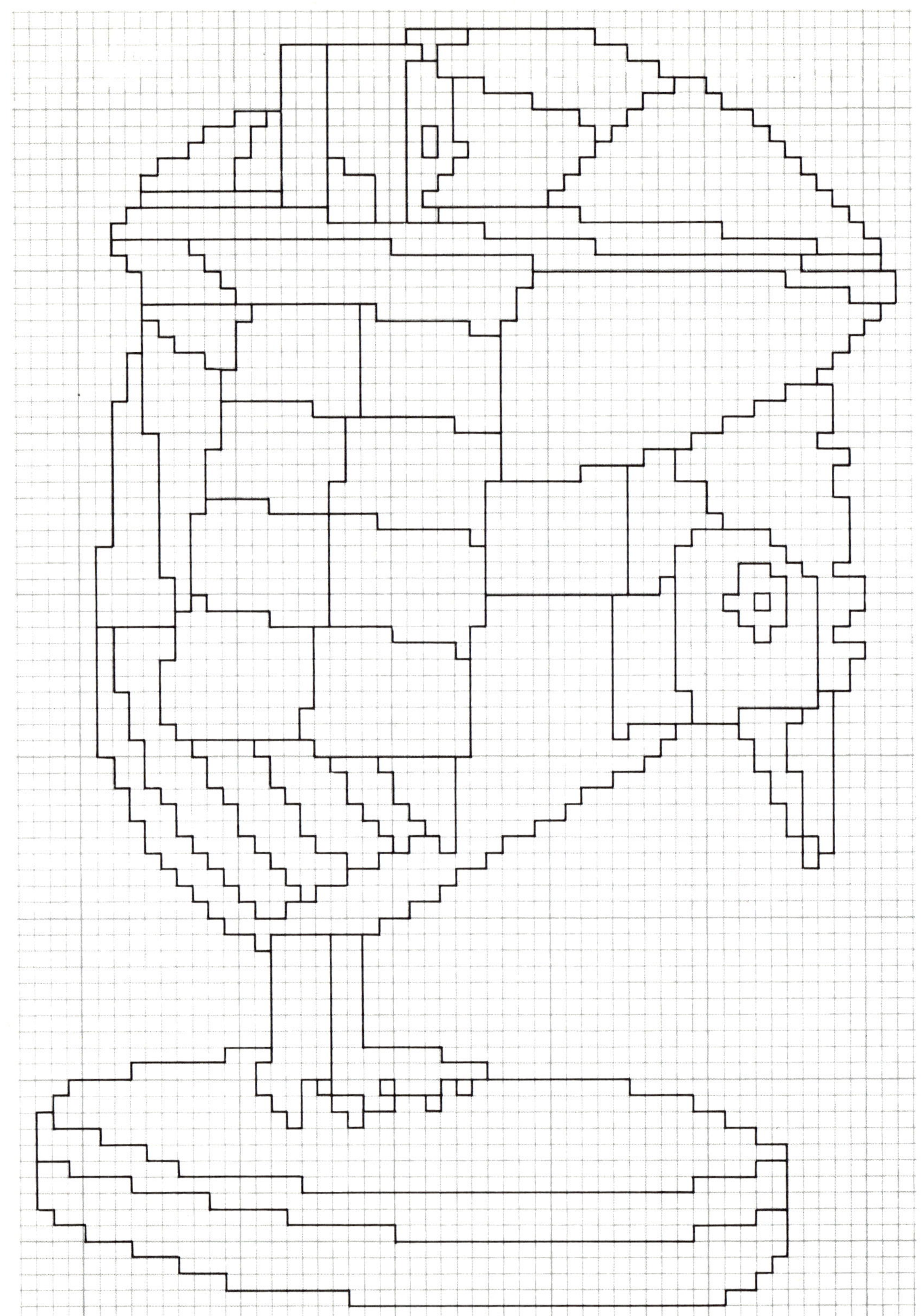

Wooden dish carved in the shape of a cock with lid placed on its comb and tail. Yoruba. Nigeria.

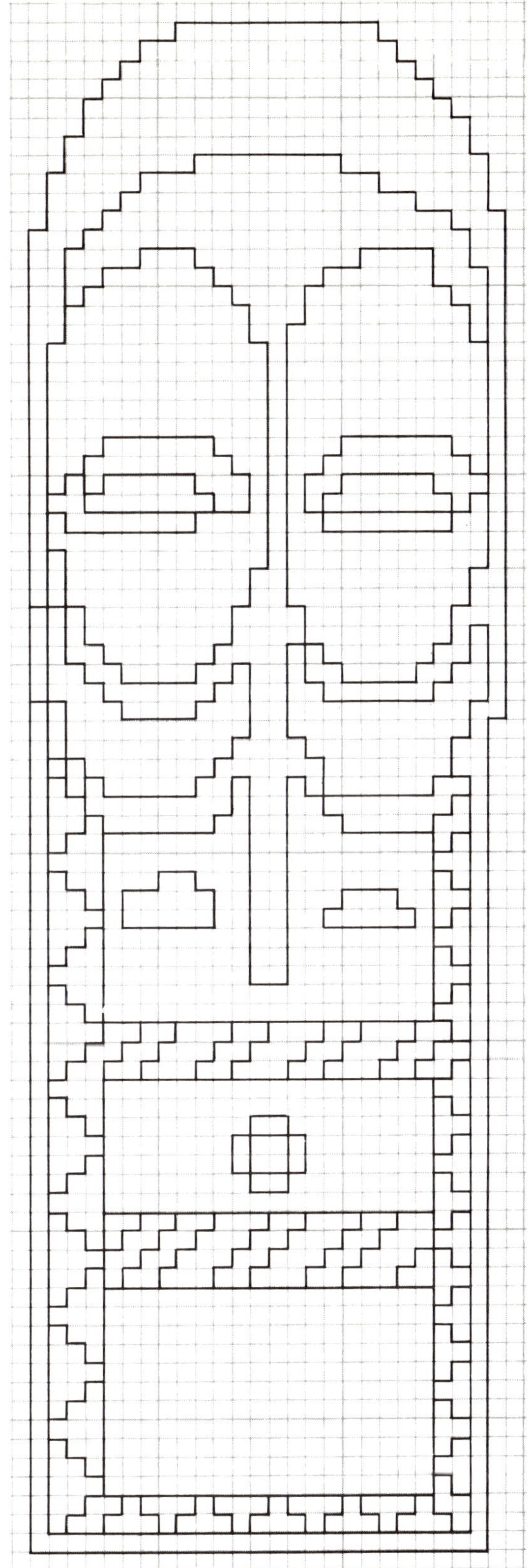

Wooden mask. Bembe. Republic of the Congo.

Carved head from divination instrument (Katora). Luba. Zaïre.

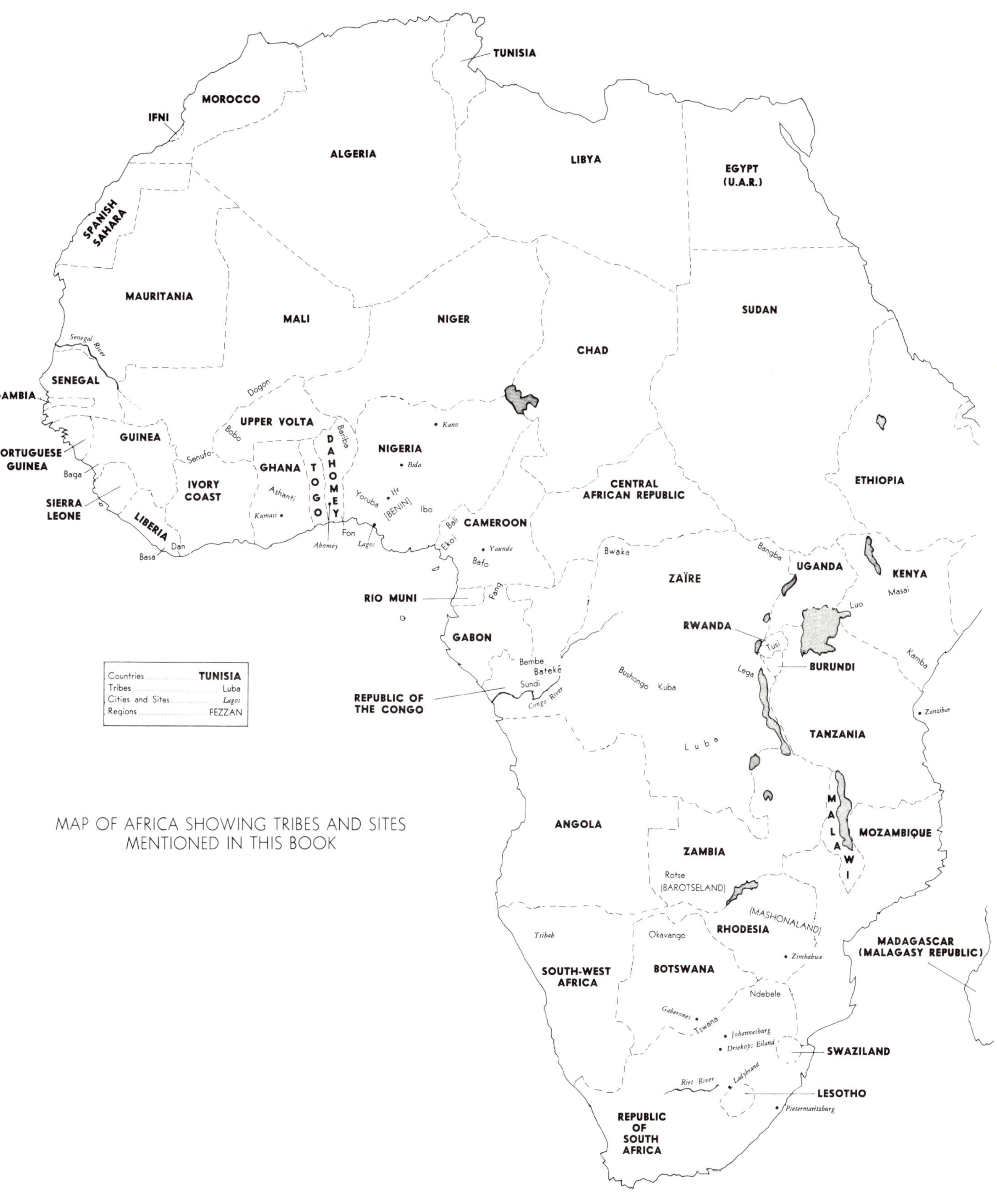

MAP OF AFRICA SHOWING TRIBES AND SITES MENTIONED IN THIS BOOK